*This journal
belongs to*

_____

Talk to Me, Jesus

HIS WORDS FOR YOU

DEVOTIONAL
JOURNAL

Belle City Gifts™
Racine, WI 53403

Belle City Gifts is an imprint of BroadStreet Publishing.
Broadstreetpublishing.com

Talk to Me, Jesus

© 2014 by BroadStreet Publishing Group, LLC.

ISBN 978-1-4245-4925-2

Journal entries composed by Marie Chapian. Author is represented by
the literary agency of Alive Communications, Inc., 7680 Goddard Street,
Suite 200, Colorado Springs, CO 80920, www.alivecommunications.com.

Design by Chris Garborg | garborgdesign.com

Printed in China.

Enter into stillness.

Tell your soul to rest a moment

while you quiet your thoughts

and give yourself permission

to be at peace in the quiet meditation

of your heart.

Listen for My voice.

I'm right here beside you

in the secret place

waiting....

I Talk to You

I talk to you day and night.
I love to talk to you,
to tell you things,
to teach you,
help you, and guide you.
When I tell you to delight yourself in Me,
it's so I can delight in you!
Talking to you is a holy journey,
beautiful and precious beyond all riches
because you are listening!
I speak to you right now.
I give you My thoughts, dearest one,
so you can embrace them into yours.
As you absorb My word,
you breathe in the breath of life.
O, it is so sweet to talk to you.

1 Timothy 4:15; Hebrews 11:3; John 12:49-50

My Words for Him

Come

Come!
Come to Me, dear one.
I hear your heart.
I hear you when you lack energy and courage.
I hear you when you are tired.
I hear you when you feel pressured
and stressed at life's demands.
I tell you, lean into Me and rest for a moment.
Breathe in My presence.

There are many demands
that you have taken onto yourself.
Too easily you are pulled out of the arms of peace and calm
and tossed into the cauldron of worry and lost sleep.
I soothe your brow.
I whisper loving words into your precious ear.
I am your safety in the storm,
I am pools of clear, cool water in the parched desert.
I am Creator of the ends of the earth. I never faint,
nor do I weary.
Take My energy and My enthusiasm into yourself.
Awaken your ear to My voice.
Blessings will overtake you.

Take this moment to pause
and consider what tasks you've taken on yourself
that you could lay at the foot of the cross.
Allow Me to take care of them without your help,
and then come to Me and rest.
Yes, rest.

Isaiah 40:28, 31; Galatians 6:9; Deuteronomy 28:2; Matthew 11:28

My Words for Him

Listen for Me Early

Listen for Me early.
When you awaken in the morning
open your eyes and your ears at the same time.
As the new day coaxes you awake,
allow Me to kiss your thoughts with My words.
Allow My voice to caress your mind with Mine.
As you enter My heart with your heart,
My thoughts will radiate and ignite your own
to a brightness that will light up the whole world.
You will be as a beacon of light on a hill.

Listen, dear one, I want you to hear My voice
at all times. I want to be able to talk to you
and know you are there.
My heart holds a heavenly kingdom
of wisdom, love, and joy to share with you
if you will listen.
I'll show you what is true, honorable, worthy of reverence;
I'll show you what is just, pure, lovely, loveable,
and what kindness looks like. I will show you
the truth! I will tell you
where virtue and excellence exist,
as well as that which is worthy of your praise.
Think and weigh what I tell you,
fix your mind on My words.

Living in Me, abiding, vitally united to Me
is what gives you wisdom.
My words remain in you
and continue to thrive and bubble up
in joyful power in you.
If you listen.
And then, dear one, as My own treasure,
created to bring delight to heaven
and the Father of heaven, you can ask Me
whatever you will and it shall be done for you.

JOHN 15:7; PHILIPPIANS 4:8; 1 CORINTHIANS 6:17

My Words for Him

Your Identity

I want you to know who you are.
 I want you to know who I am.
I want you to take what I freely give you
 and multiply it. Multiply yourself!
You have a never-ending supply of power
 and ability in you because I am in you.
I want you to see yourself as brave and indefatigable.
 I want you to see yourself as created
in My image.

I want you to see yourself
 physically strong and capable.
I am infusing strength into your cells,
 bones, and tissues.
I am in you to restore and ignite
 your spirit with enthusiasm and faith.
Trust Me. Trust Me in you.
 Trust yourself in Me.

Your identity is in Me,
 so I ask you to love how you are made,
splendid and perfect, prepared in all manner
 to express your beautiful self
in your world, and to joyfully multiply
 all that I give you.

GENESIS 1:26; ROMANS 8:29; 2 CORINTHIANS 3:18; COLOSSIANS 3:10

My Words for Him

I Have Your Future in My Hand

Your future is bright!
       I have set before you opportunities
to rise high above your current status.
       There is enormous power inside you.
Do not settle for less,
       and then later gaze about disheartened
wondering what happened
       to your promised breakthrough.
The time is now, I tell you.
       Now is the time to take hold
of the opportunities I set before you.
       Now is the time
to expand your faith and your trust in Me.

I have placed choices
       before you.
I've laid out precious stones
       for your foundation.
I've made My justice
       your measuring line.
I've given you wisdom as a co-partner.
       I've given you visions and dreams
to enlarge your understanding
       and to challenge complacency and status quo.
Nothing about Me is complacent.
       Remember, I am the potter
and you are the clay.
       I have sculpted you beautifully and perfectly
to fulfill your calling.
       I've written My name on your heart.
You are fully equipped.

JEREMIAH 29:11; 1 CHRONICLES 29:12; ISAIAH 29:16, 62:2; PSALM 25:12-13

My Words for Him

When You Are Tempted

What are the triggers that pull you away
    from Me?
What temptation can yank you
    from My arms?
What can fling you so easily
    into the abyss, and then
as I wait and reach for you, I hear your small voice,
    "Help,"
and I am there.

Recognize the temptations in advance, dear one.
These painful interruptions and road blocks
    that loom in the haven of your spiritual progress
are not accidents. They are choices.
    I tell you, listen to the small temptations
for they are the snakebites of the enemy
    and they chew at your heels to draw you
to your belly
    sorry and defeated.

I have come that you might have a big life
of abundant blessing and happiness.
    You do not have to spend your hours fighting off
demons at every turn. You can be free
    from every temptation
as you permit Me to break off every chain that binds you.
    It's a choice.

James 1:12; 1 John 1:9; Psalm 33:20; Hebrews 10:23;
Matthew 6:13, 26:41; Mark 14:38

My Words for Him

The One Who Prevails

Dearest one, enter the gates of My heart with your thankful heart;
     enter into My Presence and My courts with praise.
Be thankful! Be joyful! Joy is your eternal reality. Thankfulness
     is your heart.
A divine test is when I ask your thankful heart to rise
     and be glad in the most difficult times.
You see, your faith is precious to Me. If you could see the monuments
     built by faith in My Kingdom, you would burst forth with joy
and gratitude for the privilege of prevailing.

     Darkness cannot last. It will not last. I am Light and I have
assigned you as light in the world.
     Look at yourself.
     What do you see?
Do you see yourself as I see you?
     When you do this, you will prevail
in all tests and in all trials.

Psalm 100:4-5; 1 Corinthians 3:13; 2 Corinthians 2:14;
1 John 1:5-7; Acts 26:18

My Words for Him

I Supply All You Need

Have I not promised to take care of your needs?
I promised to grant you the wisdom and
the ability to produce wealth.
I promised to anoint you
with the capacity to perform skills
that will produce benefits beyond your expectations.
I promised you a new mindset
designed to be centered squarely on My guidance.
Therefore, I lead you forward
and give you verdant, rich soil
in which to sow your seeds of greatness.

It is My will that you prosper
in the expertise you've worked hard to develop.
I have seen your labor and your holy discipline.
Your prayers of praise and gratitude
have formed an inextinguishable luminosity
that heaven rejoices over.
Your love draws favor to you,
and to the calling I have given you to inhabit.

You have found what is more important
than yourself.
That is why you are beautiful to the world
and why I can say to you *I know you*.
You've made *Me* most important in your life,
and you've dedicated your life
and breath to Me. That is why, dear one,
you wear a crown of promise
upon your head and are clothed with resplendent favor.

Deuteronomy 29:9, 30:5; Joshua 1:7-8; Psalm 68:19;
Philippians 4:13, 19; Ephesians 1:3; 2 Timothy 4:8

My Words for Him

Be Confident

Let Me kiss you with confidence.
You are strong because I am strong.
In the inner chambers of your being,
beloved one,
I give you divine authority and aptitude
by My Spirit.
You are equipped to go forth fearlessly
in command of all I've given you to do
and be.
Deep within you is a colossal sea
of power, and it has a sound.
It is as the sound of a mighty rushing wind
drawing up inside you to do
and be
that which I have anointed you for.

Take your authority as a shield,
a weapon, and a tool
to create something beautiful for your Father in heaven.
My Holy Spirit goes before you in glorious light–
His light is like steel breaking the cobwebs of darkness.

Dearest, your strength in Me
will open sealed doors
that have not seen the sun for centuries.
You will dance on the shards of mourning with Me
and you will yank the devil's chains from the bellies
of fashionable liars, clever thieves, and unseen killers.
Together we will set naïve captives free
and gird the broken hearted with precious new-found gladness.

JOB 4:6; PSALM 65:5; EPHESIANS 3:12; HEBREWS 3:6, 14, 10:35,
ISAIAH 61:1; EZEKIEL 36:27; ACTS 2:2-4

My Words for Him

Growing Older

You'll bear much fruit in old age, dear one.
  I have called you to produce greatness
in all your years on earth.
   You'll be as a fresh bloom on the rose vine yearly,
and you'll continue to flourish in Me.
Never speak of growing old and weary.
   If I haven't put the words in your heart,
don't speak them.
   My words are life and abundance,
so proclaim My words to yourself
   and to the world!
Fruitfulness, longevity,
   strength, creativity,
joyfulness, peace,
   abundance, and prosperity–
these are what I have called you to
   and given you.

Relish in My gifts.
Relish in the power My Holy Spirit gives you
   and your youth renewed as the eagle's.
My eyes are on the faithful of the earth
   so you may remain moment by moment
with Me,
listening for My voice,
   and loving My favor.
Listen to Me. The children of My servants
   will continue
and their descendants will be established before Me.
   This is My promise to you.

Psalms 92:2, 14, 101:6, 102:28

My Words for Him

I Promise

How many times have I whispered courage
          into your ear? How many times
have I held you in My arms and kissed your dear heart
          with My heart? I love you, darling one.
I love you.
          Nothing can separate us. Nothing ever will.
You are Mine and I have you ever
          as the apple of My eye. Can you understand that?

Oh beloved,
          today lean your heart
and your mind on Me.
          Tell Me your thoughts, your dreams,
your desires. I love to hear your thoughts.
          I love it when you come to Me
with your deepest wants and hopes.
          I know you long for more
than what you have at this time
          and I am with you to make it possible
for you to expand, grow,
          and draw to yourself everything you dream of
and long for.
          I promise.

1 Kings 8:56; Romans 4:21; Deuteronomy 31:6; Psalms 48:9, 119:59

My Words for Him

In Training

Consider yourself in training.
   When your spiritual muscles are tight and unflexed,
They require gentle stretching.
   I love it when you discipline your spiritual muscles,
not neglecting your higher calling to be strong in Me.
   Just as you won't enjoy the thrill of physical feats
without training and discipline,
   you won't discover the joy of spiritual fitness
   without spiritual training.
This requires time spent with Me, partnering with Me
   as I guide you into proper holy alignment
and build your muscular ability
   beyond that which you are capable of on your own.

Take one step at a time
   drawing closer and closer to Me and My word,
understanding and accepting your new life.
   You are learning day by day to walk by beautiful faith
and not by your physical sight. Watch your spiritual muscles
   become stronger and stronger!
And then, swift and smooth, you run,
   not on blistered hopes and aching schemes for a better life,
but aimed sure and steady on a true course,
   joining the race that has already been won for you.

2 Timothy 2:15, 4:15; 2 Peter 1:5-8; Hebrews 12:1

My Words for Him

Very Good

I love how you make things beautiful, dear one.
　　　I love how you can turn ordinary things
into things of beauty.
　　　You are My heart
because I love to turn ashes to beauty
　　　and mourning to joy.
You do the same, My dearest one.

And another thing,
　　　I love your love for color
and art and nature
　　　because I love color and art and nature, too.
When you thank Me for trees
　　　and sigh how magnificent is the sunrise,
I sigh, too.
　　　Remember, I said, "It is good,"
when I created the earth
　　　for you to love and care for.
But even more,
　　　when I created you
and told you to be fruitful and multiply,
　　　I sighed twice and said it is VERY good.

Genesis 1:26-31; Matthew 5:13-16, 7:18

My Words for Him

Called to Ride Out the Storm

Climb into faith today.
　　　Thrust your entire body, soul, and spirit
into the ocean of power called Faith.
　　　No storm will ever swallow you
in its squall.
　　　Believe today that you can do all things
through your Savior who strengthens you.
　　　Lean into Me and feel Me breathe into you
with My words.
You are strong in Me
　　　and in the power of My might.

You are not like the faithless
　　　who faint at the sound of trouble's thunder.
You are not like those who cringe at the sight of
　　　roiling black clouds and blades of lightning.
No, dear one, you are called to ride out every storm
　　　like an eagle who flies high above the chaos.
You're called to rise above the blinding blizzards of life
　　　that assail the human spirit.
I love your courage,
　　　your ability to possess beautiful calm
in the midst of bedlam.
　　　No trial is too much for you because
you trust Me.
　　　I caress you today in My love and joy.

Hebrews 11:1-2, 6; Psalm 103:5; James 1:6;
Isaiah 40:31; Matthew 8:26

My Words for Him

Black Waters of Worry

I see you when your mind floats
in the black, infested waters of worry.
Dearest child, you are too easily persuaded
to worry about the things
over which you have no control.
My will is that you train your thoughts
to think My thoughts, and that you permit Me
to manage what you cannot.
Do not negate the power of your prayers.
I hear you
and I answer!

Do I heal? Do I deliver?
Do I patiently guide you?
Have I not told you to pursue the Kingdom of God
to receive all the blessings that yearn
to be added to you?
Is My arm shortened
that I'm unable to reach far enough to save you from what
worries you?
Oh dear one, allow Me to renew your mind
so all your anxious thoughts will become heaven-kissed.
Do not resist.

Romans 8:6; Philippians 2:5; Isaiah 55:9, 59:1;
Psalms 40:5, 17, 139:17; Jeremiah 29:11

My Words for Him

Who Are You?

I, who have formed the eye, can I not see?
I instruct the nations, darling one,
        shall I not correct you, also?
I am clothed in majesty
        and I have girded Myself with strength.
I want you to gird yourself in My strength
        which is tried and tested and perfect,
and yours.
        I am the One who teaches humankind
knowledge and wisdom.
        It takes a person of spiritual strength
to choose knowledge and wisdom
above all else.
        All of heaven opens its arms to you
and you become a pillar,
        unshakeable, unmovable,
steadfast, and abounding
        in wonderful works.

I've called you to prosper
        in all areas of your life;
your thoughts, ideas, desires, hopes.
        I called you to prosper physically,
to strengthen the muscles
        and joints of your dear body
which is My temple.
        I've called you to prosper
in your relationships
        with other believers
so that united you'll produce much golden fruit
        which you couldn't do alone.
I've called you to prosper in your creativity
        to bring forth that which has never been seen before.
I hear and see all, and as you listen
        to My leading and allow Me
to correct and keep you on the right path,
        you'll find nothing is impossible to you.

2 Chronicles 20:6; Psalms 24:10, 93:1-2; Jeremiah 9:24;
Deuteronomy 29:9; 1 Chronicles 22:13; Matthew 17:20

My Words for Him

In Me

When you feel complete in Me
you'll no longer be afraid
of My holy discipline;
you'll no longer feel punished by discipline.
No, darling, you'll feel relieved and grateful
at being made to go forward
on the right path.
When you choose your own ways of doing things
and ignoring My word,
you'll grow hard on yourself
because you'll never be good enough
or do well enough to please yourself.
You may rationalize your faults,
sins, and shortcomings,
but your rationalizations won't satisfy you.
Your self-demands will increase
and your need for relief
from your self-imposed pressures will increase.
Is this when you'll return to Me?

I welcome you with open arms.
I am a forgiving God.
Deny yourself the indulgence of wasted time
and come close to Me.
I am the Vine
and you are the delightful twiggy growth
shooting out from Me.
Never be afraid of My discipline.
Discipline means
you are being made to share My glory.
If you are to be like Me,
certain efforts have to be made by you.
This is a continual process,
and one we share together.
I am leading you now to a higher place
in the Kingdom of God, beloved.
Don't resist.

Colossians 2:10; Job 36:10; Deuteronomy 30:3; Luke 1:38, 19:10; Romans 1:20; Proverbs 20:6; Matthew 16:25, 25:34

My Words for Him

_____

_____

_____

_____

_____

_____

_____

_____

_____

_____

_____

_____

_____

_____

_____

_____

_____

_____

_____

_____

_____

The Broken Heart

When your heart is broken and
      you feel betrayed, deceived;
I tell you, rise up to the challenge.
      Rise up strong.
Set your face like a flint and don't let the enemy discourage
      and shake you. You are not weak.
You were born to handle trials.
      These minor betrayals will fall away from you
like gnats from the flanks of stallions.
      You are brave and courageous and wise.
This is a minor disruption in your pursuit of excellence.
      Don't dwell on evil.
Keep your eyes off the lie and look to Me.
      Vengeance is Mine.
      I will surge light into the blackness of evil intent,
and your integrity shall be as a beacon.
      Act in love, for love is My heart.
Behave with wisdom, for wisdom is My name.
      Your integrity has not been compromised.
Can you walk away?
      Can you walk away with your head held high
and your integrity intact?
      I say yes, yes you can.

NAHUM 1:7; 2 CORINTHIANS 4:8, 9; PSALM 138:7;
ISAIAH 43:2; ROMANS 12:19

My Words for Him

I'll Never Leave You

I will never let you go.
There is no place too far away for Me to reach you.
You may run to the uttermost parts of the earth
and I'll find you there.
You may bury yourself in the sands of work,
shroud yourself in worldly pleasures
and I am there.
You may roam the world seeking adventure,
scour the seven seas in search of exploits,
journey the continents in pursuit of new frissons and thrills–
you take Me with you.
If you are overwhelmed
in your quest of higher learning,
I am here beside you.
No distance or pursuit can keep Me from you.

If you entertain guilt and shame,
I am there.
Drenched in sorrow, I am there.
Angry, out of sorts, I am there.
Frustrated, upset, I am there.
Nervous, fretful, I am there.
You can't escape Me.
Nothing can separate us.
I never turn My head from you.
Your wants and needs are important to Me,
so let these words resound in your consciousness:
I will never leave you nor forsake you.
You are Mine!

John 10:27-29; 2 Thessalonians 3:3;
Jude 1:24-25; Romans 8:38-39

My Words for Him

I Know You've Been Hurt

You worry because of past experiences when you've been hurt.
　　　You worry you'll be hurt again.
You're afraid I won't keep My promises to protect you
　　　and watch over you.
You're afraid you'll slip out of My sight–
　　　not a chance!
Every hair on your head is numbered.
　　　You are always before me.
I have you imprinted on the palm of My hand.

See Me as your strength, your strong tower.
　　　See your Lord and Savior surrounding you
with wisdom and discernment to keep you
　　　from leaping into miry clay and hasty judgments.
When your feet are situated solidly on the rock
　　　where I've placed you,
you have a clean vision before you.
　　　The skies are clear.
Why do I promise to set you on a high place?
　　　So you can see clearly!
Trust My Spirit within you.
　　　You will never be happy until
you free yourself from the fear of being hurt
　　　to having full confidence in the wisdom
I freely give you.
　　　I will protect you and watch over you
all the days of your life.

2 Corinthians 4:9; Psalms 27:10, 91:14-15;
Isaiah 49:15-16; Deuteronomy 31:6; John 14:1

My Words for Him

Your Finest Hour

This is your finest hour. I have prepared you for this hour.
Put on your courage.

Be steadfast, unmovable, abounding in the work I've
called you to.

My Presence goes before you.

Take hold of the task without trepidation.
Never be afraid because I will always accomplish
that which I ordain. You will bear much splendid fruit
and you will complete all I have required of you,
plus more.

You are a chosen delight to Me and to the heavenly host
that surrounds and helps you.

Be aware of the angels helping you and cheering for you.

Angels are very happy beings. Created in love,
as you are, but never wearing the covering of
doubting human flesh. My angels know only happiness.
Welcome them.

Anoint your heart with the oil of gladness
and breathe in the aroma of complete confidence
in My ability. To face a task I give you without confidence
is like a gift standing alone and forlorn without a giver.
How can there be a gift without a giver?

Have confidence, dear one, join the celebration
of angels and awaken new trust in your heart.

This is your finest hour. Grasp it with joy.
You are not alone.

1 Corinthians 15:58; Isaiah 40:31, 41:10; Philippians 4:13;
Ephesians 6:10; Psalms 4:7, 30:11, 45:7; Hebrews 13:5

My Words for Him

Safe in My Arms

No matter where you are
and no matter what is going on around you,
        you are safe in Me.
My arms are your refuge and your home.
        I am continually reminding you of this.
My arms never tire of holding you.
        Never, never, never.

During the day
        remember the everlasting arms of God
are holding you.
During the night think of your Savior
        holding you tight in His everlasting arms.

Be careful not to stumble into muddy puddles of strife.
        The mud of strife
will cloud your eyes,
        and the granules will stick in your teeth.
Your heart hungers for oxygen,
        and strife will choke your breath.
Dearest one, it's time to enlarge
        the walls of your understanding
and permit your soul to expand in knowledge
        of My love for you.
Then your entire being will radiate with the light of confidence.

Why are you safe and secure, beloved one?
        Because your home is in My arms.

DEUTERONOMY 33:27; PSALM 40:2; ISAIAH 63:1; LUKE 19:10

My Words for Him

A Time to Rest

I am calling you to depart from your labors for a moment and rest.

I love you and I love to refresh and restore you with a quiet time of repose. As you breathe in My Spirit, I will transport you to peace and renewal. Let Me kiss your brow, caress your neck.

I want you to see and know how good it is in My garden of calm stillness. I want you to see how sweet it is when you allow My Spirit to embrace your mind and body with new life.

Oh, beautiful child of Mine, pause and rest for a moment with Me.

Be refreshed and invigorated, for I equip you with all you need for every task.

There is no task I give you that you are not equipped to fulfill. I am the giver of strength, all energy originates in Me. I am the giver of wisdom and courage, and I give you all you need. Rest now in your strength. Rest in your talents and gifts, knowing you will succeed in all that I have called you to do.

Isaiah 11:2, 26:3, 30:15; Jeremiah 31:3; John 14:27;
2 Corinthians 9:8; Psalm 68:19; Philippians 1:6; Romans 11:33

My Words for Him

Success

Breathe in My approval at this moment.
    I want to give you all that is possible
of My love and glory at this moment.
    I want to fulfill you
with a sense of true belonging
    to what is greater than yourself.
I want you to feel the warming sensation
    in your heart of being completely loved.
Beautiful child of Mine, in My eyes you are a success.
    When you came to Me
surrendering your life to Me,
    a successful person was born.
You can do all things through Me,
    for I give you strength,
I give you fortitude,
    I give you courage,
I give you stick-to-it-ness,
    I give you perseverance.
Dearest one, I give you a peaceful heart
    in the midst of uncertainty.
You do not have to prove anything to anyone.
    Do your work and be glad in it.
I am with you.
    Be who I have created you to be,
and do what I have created you to do.

ROMANS 4:21; 2 CORINTHIANS 1:20; MARK 9:23, 11:24;
JOHN 1:12, 14:13, 15:16; SONG OF SONGS 8:6-7A

My Words for Him

Don't Be Hard on Yourself

I tell you, rise up, My lovely one.
        Put away the darkness.
Be at peace with yesterday,
        and look at the hope I set before you now.
I am right here, closer than you think,
        calling you, holding you,
whispering in your ear, directly into your heart.
So many things in your life unnerve you, upset you,
and these are the darts that cause you to either shrink back
or rise up in strength.
        I tell you, My lovely one, your life is good,
and I will always bring you through the storms
        confronting you.
And when the darts fly, I am there
        to take them on My body before they strike you.
Don't you see?
        All that comes at you to cause you worry and stress
        I have taken on Myself.
Every step you take, you take with Me.
        When you are weary or uncertain,
I pick you up in My arms and I place you in a safe place.
I tell you, My lovely one,
        stop putting yourself down.
You are hard on yourself
        because you listen to false voices around you.
Listen for My voice, My beautiful one.
        I am putting a new song in you.
I am bringing you to the pinnacle of your destiny
        where you will shine for years to come
for the dark, despairing world you left behind to see.
That world will have no hold on you
        because you have left its influence
and its clawing at your flesh.
        You are walking in the freedom
I died to give you freely, freely.
        Just take, My lovely one, take all I give you.

Psalm 121:1-2; Hebrews 4:15-16; 1 Peter 5:7; Colossians 1:13; John 16:13; Romans 8:31; Matthew 24:35

My Words for Him

The Secret Place

Is that you My darling one,
> dwelling in the secret place of the Most High?
Is that you making your home in the shadow of the Almighty?
> Is it you who has made Me your refuge
and your fortress?
> Am I the One you trust?
Is it you safely tucked under My wings?
> Yes, and I feel you snuggled next to Me,
warm and safe, our hearts pulsing together,
> you, comforted in your place of refuge.

Have you made My truth your shield and buckler?
> Have you made Me your protection and
your strength?
> Do you see that it is I who delivers you
> from the snare of the fowler
and the perilous pestilences?
> Do you see there is no cause to worry, ever,
about anything?
> Ah, dearest one, never be afraid of what appears to be
the terror by night,
> nor of the arrow that flies by day.
Never fret about the diseases, plagues, and epidemics
> that stalk about in darkness,
nor of the destruction that lays waste at noonday.
> O, never!
There will always be persecutions and trials,
> but you'll see a thousand fall at your side
> and ten thousand at your right hand,
but you will not be singed by their fire.
> The wicked have their reward.
But you have made Me your dwelling place,
> and no evil can touch you here with Me!

Psalm 91:1-16

My Words for Him

Created to Know Me

You were created to know Me
       and to glorify God with your life.
Be careful you don't wear yourself out
       doing that which appears to be good,
but is not what you are called to do.
       You can't fulfill the calling of another,
and the work you do in their stead
       will steal your time and your energy,
and eventually you'll become frustrated
       and over-extended.
There is a time to work and a time to rest
       from your work.
If you do more than you are called to do,
       where will you find rest?

Come apart
       and allow Me to breathe new vision
into your awareness.
       The vision I give you is
for your life alone.
       I don't give you the vision for another's life
because I am a personal Savior.
       I speak individually to My children.
Your vision for your life is yours,
       nobody else's.
Your calling is yours,
       nobody else's.
Both your vision and your calling
       are holy and impenetrable golden darts
firing forth toward eternity,
       as every task I give you
has eternity as its heart.
       Today consider what is yours to accomplish
on your schedule
       and what belongs to someone else.

1 Corinthians 1:27-28; Psalms 31:3; 37:23; Isaiah 48:17;
Job 2:5; Matthew 5:8; John 3:27, 16:14-15

My Words for Him

When Problems Beset You

When you think you should not have problems
      to contend with,
you're thinking your own thoughts , not Mine.
      When you think you should never
have to confront evil,
      you are thinking your own thoughts,
not Mine.
      When you think life in Me should be pain-free
without serious trials,
      you have missed My mind.
Darling one, I don't erase the trials;
      I empower you to face them
and overcome!

Don't forget
      I have given My angels charge over you
to keep you in all your ways.
      You're not alone.
Never alone!
      My angels bear you up
and I empower you to stomp
      on the swarming beasts of defeat
that assail you.
      I know you love Me,
and I love your love.
      That is why I have set My perfect love upon you
and continue to deliver you from harm.
      I set you on a high place
because you adore My name,
      and each time you call on Me
I will answer you.
      Do you understand?
I am with you in every trouble!
      I am your deliverer, sent by God
to deliver you from all bondage.
      You'll live long with a satisfied life.

PSALMS 32:8, 91:1-6; PROVERBS 3:5-6, 6:22-23

My Words for Him

Ever Stronger

I strengthen you on the bed of languishing.
I lift you out of torpid sorrow.
No worry shall possess you
and hold you down. I have planted you
in a place of safety and peace.
You shall not feed the wolves of depression
that harass you. I am your Lord
and I save you from yourself and from
all your weaknesses. You are not deficient in Me.
You are a powerful overcomer
and a beautiful child in My Kingdom.

Can you see yourself as I see you?

When you begin to doubt and fret,
turn to Me and listen to My words
of encouragement and love.
I see you as a mighty warrior of valor
in My Kingdom. I have called you!
You are My family!

Never doubt Me.
Never doubt yourself.
You are everything I have called you to be.
I give you many challenges,
and I give you many joyful tasks. Enter each
with expectation and delight.
Never doubt I say; *never doubt.*

Proverbs 3:5-6; Psalm 55:22; Isaiah, 40:29, 41:10, 50:7;
Philippians 4:6-7

My Words for Him

_____
_____
_____
_____
_____
_____
_____
_____
_____
_____
_____
_____
_____
_____
_____
_____
_____
_____
_____
_____
_____
_____

The Extra Mile

I love your heart and I love how you cling to Me,
  refusing to be blown down from the tower of faith.
Stand fast in the storm assailing around you
  because you are solidly fixed on a high place
where nothing can daunt you.
  The extra mile I have assigned you
can only be completed in the power of My Spirit.
  Your courage lives in the rock-hard integrity
of your faith.
  But there's more.

Even as you carry on in courage and boldness, dear one,
  reach inside for your cheerful heart.
Allow yourself to chuckle at the sound of the storm surrounding you
  with a joyful awakening inside, as though a flower has opened
in the hurricane of your emotions.
  Again I tell you, let nothing daunt you.
Face the storm with a smile and the force of the winds
  will diminish.
The extra mile is a gift I have assigned you
  because as you hold steady and sure on your tower of faith,
I want to see your sweet, trusting smile.
  I want to feel your heart beat with Mine in perfect peace.

1 Timothy 4:7-8, Psalm 31:24; Matthew 5:41, 28:18;
2 Corinthians 5:7; Ezekiel 36:27; Zechariah 4:6

My Words for Him

Toward Tomorrow

I know that sometimes you think
            the best has passed you by.
This is not true.
            The best might have been for a time
as you perceived it, but more than best
            is yet to come. You have missed nothing.
The past has been a stepping stone
            to your bright future.
Stop looking at years.
            Look at Me.

This is not the time for you to withdraw.
            This is the time for you
to move forward. This is the time
            for you to plunge ahead
fearlessly and bravely.
            You are My strong one. Go! I say, go!

Don't hold back.
            I am blessing and anointing you.
You have nothing whatsoever to fear.
            This is your time to break through the gates
of darkness and plunge into glorious light,
            not only for you, but for many others.
I give you everything you need.
            Now it's up to you.

2 Chronicles 32:7; Ezra 10:4; Luke 12:32;
Hebrews 4:14; Deuteronomy 11:26-28

My Words for Him

Love Yourself

You are never to put yourself down.
>Never say to yourself, "Woe is me."

No woe is you or yours.
>I am your joy

and the lifter of your head.
>I am your glory.

>I am your shield.

I save you from woe and finding fault
>with yourself.

But this you must understand:
>I save you from your self-denigrations

and every woeful misery
>when you run headlong into My arms.

Take My word as your shield
>and your strength.

I am your strong tower.
>When you run to Me, you're safe

from your degrading self-talk.
>I call you wonderfully made

and beautiful.
>When your mind is locked inside

the fortress of My mind,
>your thoughts become Mine

and become like pure golden arrows
>to attack every lie

that besieges and demeans you.
>The truth of My Word

and My endless love for you
>will eradicate the muck

of self-pity and oppression.

ECCLESIASTES 3:11; SONG OF SONGS 4:16, 6:4

My Words for Him

Never Give Up

Beloved, I am with you. I will fulfill My word concerning you.
I will fulfill every promise I have made to you.
I cannot lie. My word to you in this hour is to stand strong.
I am with you.

I am calling you to stand strong by the power of My Spirit within you.
The storms of life prove the power of God within you.
You have the power to overcome, to rise up
and prove My Word and My promises.

You have the power to triumph in all things
because I live in you.
You are My treasure and My delight. Listen to your heart.
Believe My Word and speak the truth into the
atmosphere around you.

Let your mind and your mouth be filled with the glorious truth
and with the power of My Word,
for great is your reward.

Isaiah 42:2-3a; Psalm 66:8-10; Romans 8:35-37

My Words for Him

Who Do You Say That I Am?

Darling one, where do you go when you have a serious need?
Who loves to answer that need?
Who doesn't judge you for whatever you ask?
Who tells you to ask whatever you will and it'll be done for you?
Who is always there for you without an appointment?
Who always listens to your problems no matter what time of day or night?
Where does your help come from?
Who lifts you up and vindicates you?
Who is always here beside you, covering you, protecting you, embracing you in perfect love?
Who calls you beloved from holy lips?
Who crowns you with loving-kindness and tender mercies?
Who heals all your diseases?
Who renews your youth like the eagle's?
When the world rejects you, who picks you up and smothers you with kisses?
Who has called you with an everlasting love?
Who loved and desired you so deeply that He died for you?
Who longs to give you a rich and meaningful life?
Who cares about every aspect of your day?
Who loves to surround you with blessings?
Who has granted goodness and mercy to follow you all the days of your life?
Who has assigned angels to watch over and protect you?
Who wants you to learn His love language and speak it fluently?
Who wants you to live in His love?
Who wants to have a love conversation with you right now?

1 Peter 9:11; Psalm 103:3; 2 Corinthians 3:18; Deuteronomy 33:27; Luke 19:10; Philippians 2:9-11; Romans 5:8

My Words for Him

Shining in Light

Come into the light with Me
    knowing you are loved and safe.
Be kind to yourself.
    Be tender-hearted, kind, and merciful
toward yourself
    as I am merciful toward you.
I know you have suffered,
    and I know your hurts.
I tell you, darling one,
    your afflictions produce for you
an eternal weight of glory.
    Let Me take you by the hand
and empower you to rise up
    beautiful in your strength.
Hold My hand as together
    we whisk the past from your shoulders
as it floats like dust
    into heaven's healing arms,
and at last empties out into
    sweet painlessness.

Pain is temporary and joy is eternal.
    I have given you joy
to bask in now, today.
    Find Me today in joy. Be surprised,
be refreshed and gladdened.
    Look for Me in the morning of your life
and you will find Me.
    I'm there for you.
    I am there and there
and there.
    And darling one, I am smiling.

JOHN 8:12, 12:46; 1 THESSALONIANS 5:5; ISAIAH 54:10;
2 CORINTHIANS 4:17; ISAIAH 60:1; NEHEMIAH 8:10

My Words for Him

The Unknown Factor

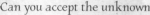

Can you accept the unknown
  when I call you to step out in faith?
Can you bravely move ahead
  when chosen for what seems uncertain?
I give you new opportunities to take hold of,
  for when I call you to a higher place in Me,
I will open doors you haven't entered.

Faith has no fear, but doubt is fashioned in fear.
If you know it is I who guides you toward fresh beginnings
and new opportunities,
  what is there to fear?
It is difficult, dear one, to press through the monumental doors
  I open for you when you are wavering
on wobbling knees and blinded by fear
  that maybe things won't "work out."

Your calling is a high calling in Me.
  Pray in My name that you'll be led by My Spirit only,
and proclaim your divinely appointed position
  as a mighty person of faith.
Remember, the one who holds back receives little.
  The one who advances bravely through the doors I open
receives all.

Hebrews 11:1-2, 16; Revelation 3:8; Isaiah 41:3;
Matthew 7:7; 1 Timothy 6:12; Luke 12:48

My Words for Him

Priorities

What are your priorities today?
        What will you focus on
in our time together today?
        I am here when you come to Me
with your plans and ideas
        and your needs and wants.
Talk to Me
        and I will talk to you.

People will come and go in your life.
        Success is temporary, riches fleeting,
but I am from everlasting to everlasting
        and your eternal self is locked in Me.
I am yours forever,
        and what concerns you
concerns Me.

Mark your priorities.
        Beware of the temptation
to use your time
on those things that are not your priority.
        Beware of exhausting yourself
on that which is not central
        to your high calling each day.
The smallest task can be the most rewarding
        when it is priority.
Not all priorities need be large tasks or duties.
        Some are the sweet, gentle, small acts
that create heaven wherever you are.

EPHESIANS 4:32, 20:12; ISAIAH 54:14-17; PSALM 119:165;
1 CORINTHIANS 10:12-13; PROVERBS 31:26

My Words for Him

Your Story

I love how you tell others about the past
when you were lost without Me,
    and how you found the meaning of life
when you gave yourself to Me. You share your story
    and many are touched at the miracles you have known
and the miracle you now live. I want you to know
    that I love to grant you miracles. Trust Me
to do the miraculous.
    I have purged iniquity from your heart and
I have removed your sins as far as the East is from the West.
    No forgiven sin remains before My face.

Forgiveness is the chief of the glorious gifts I offer!

    You, darling one, have gained a place in the center of
My heart,
and I have many, many gifts for you. I've given you
    wholeness and purpose, peace,
but don't forget healing.
    Your story encourages and lifts and heals. I pursue
the broken mind and the broken heart, so take your healing gift
    and speak into the lives of the hurting
with courage and confidence.
    I will do the miracles.

1 John 4:14; Ephesians 2:4-5; Romans 10:8-10;
Matthew 3:11; John 14:12-14

My Words for Him

Consider Yourself Blessed

I knew you
        before you were in your mother's womb,
and I loved you.
        Come into the terrain of My thoughts
and intentions. Step into My Kingdom
        so richly populated with courage, strength, goodness,
blessings, honor, favor, and overcoming triumph.
        This is your life!
I've called you out of the traps of worry and fear
        and placed you in the sound atmosphere
of My presence. It is time
        to remove periodic patchy faith, tension, discord,
and those things in your life that intrude on your
        conscious awareness and intimate connection with Me.

When you ask for forgiveness, you are forgiven.
        I took your sins on Me. I paid for your brilliant life.
You are embraced by acceptance.

My love saturates all of you.
        Allow My Spirit to pulsate at the midpoint of your being
because the sweet ecstasy of our union transforms you and
        elevates you above the thick fog of the world's troubles.
I have created a new heart in you because you asked.
        I covered you with the shadow of My hand
and planted My words in your mouth.
        Consider yourself *blessed*.

JEREMIAH 1:5, 24:7; PSALMS 5:12, 18:35, 24:17, 68:19; JOSHUA 1:9;
2 SAMUEL 22:31, 33; ACTS 5:31; ISAIAH 49:2; MATTHEW 6:33

My Words for Him

Happy Is a Choice

It's easy to become discouraged.
　　　Teaching yourself to be happy is a process
worked together with Me and My Holy Spirit.
　　　You must combat the bears of defeat,
self-pity, anger, and gloom
　　　to achieve lasting happiness.
The world is not your enemy.
　　　Your current situation is not your problem.
Family and friends are not the cause of your discontent.
　　　You are.
You alone hold the key
　　　to unlocking the gates of a truly happy life.
I can't do it for you.
　　　You must choose.

So choose today whom you'll continue to serve
　　　with your thoughts and plans.
Will you be prey for your own devices and imaginations?
　　　I tell you, I am here to renew your mind,
to give you a new heart of flesh,
　　　to raise you up
and bless your every breath because
　　　I want you to reach your full potential in Me.
I want you to be happy.
　　　But you must teach yourself
to choose.

PROVERBS 1:5, 3:13, 23-24; DEUTERONOMY 30:19;
JOSHUA 24:15

My Words for Him

Possibilities from Heaven

I send you possibilities from heaven today.
These possibilities are unfinished tasks
and open doors for you to enter,
explore, and complete in My name.
I don't ask you to sweat out a task on your own.
I am your Divine Enabler who grants you possibilities,
and I empower you to enlarge them.
You have within you the authority
to create greatness on the earth.

I have given you the earth as a gift
and an assignment to tend and care for.
When you reach out from your weakness
into the powerhouse of My strength
to touch your world,
you are fulfilling your assignment.
And it is beautiful!

MATTHEW 19:26; LUKE 18:27; MARK 9:23; JAMES 2:14;
HEBREWS 11:6; 1 CORINTHIANS 1:27; JOEL 3:10

My Words for Him

Free to Love Your Life

You possess My heart.
I have freely given to you
    because you are valuable to Me.
You are worth giving My life for
    and worth loving.
I have made a place for you in My heart.

    "Oh no," you say, "I am not worthy,"
and I must remind you there is no distance
    of decadence beyond My reach.

Do you not recognize
    how I love you?
You are pure in My sight,
    forgiven and cleansed
and free to love your life.
    I want you to enjoy
the myriad gifts I bring you daily,
    each as a kiss from heaven
tenderly blessed by your Heavenly Father.
    Today you are surrounded by joy in the spirit realm.
Be grateful.

JOHN 3:16, 15:11; 1 JOHN 4:8-10; GALATIANS 5:1;
EPHESIANS 1:13-14; 1 SAMUEL 16:7

My Words for Him

The Patient One

Patience is the muscle and fiber
    of spiritual power.
The challenges of a difficult path
    are a journey of triumph.
I conquer all weakness
    and in Me there is no helplessness
and no turning back.
    Dear one, have patience in the time that
achievement requires.
    Find happiness in the wait
    and the upward climb
which calls for resilience.
    But oh how your soul expands
in such divine labors.
    I place a blue ribbon of excellence
on your chest.
    Strong, strong, I say,
you are ready for anything
    when you climb the mountains
I put before you. Strong in character,
    full and complete,
nothing will deter, nor defeat you, dear one.
    Nothing.

Psalms 27:14, 40:1; Hebrews 6:12, 12:1;
James 1:3-4; Colossians 1:1

My Words for Him

Come Laugh with Me

Come laugh with Me.
      Let us find something very good today
to laugh together over.
      How about, for instance, we laugh at
how the devil failed to trip you up,
      and My angels caught you in their
beautiful arms.
      See how safe you are in Me?
You can laugh with genuine delight
      in the safe arms of your Heavenly Father.
Beloved, I love to laugh.
      In heaven there is much joy and laughter.
Angels love to giggle. You can hear them if you
      listen with your spiritual ears.

The gift of true delight
      is one of My best gifts.
Treasure My gift of delight.
      Do you remember My words, "Delight in the Lord
and He will give you the desires of your heart?"
      To be truly delighted
is to be fully present in Me.
      Heaven sings all around you in such delight,
your mind and heart resound with vibrating oneness
      with heaven's purposes and desires.
Delighted in Me, your heart is My heart and
      all your desires are fulfilled.

PSALMS 23:6, 27:1, 37:4; 2 THESSALONIANS 5:16-18;
JOHN 15:11; JUDE 1:24-25; ROMANS 8:32

My Words for Him

I See Your Kindness

What small act of kindness can you do today
that will bring heaven into someone's life?
Can you smile, bless, and give a cheerful word to the
unlovely?
Can you love a friend who has wronged you?
Can you lift up the spirits of a downtrodden soul?
Can you show kindness when the rest of the world spews disdain?
There are small acts of kindness,
but there also are those acts where you must reach
into the muted areas of your soul
to show mercy where you don't think mercy is merited.
There is a fleshly part of you that would judge
before showing mercy or kindness.
Can you look into those regions of your soul
and send the balm of forbearance into each layer?

One day you'll judge the angels,
but today, dear one, you are called
to shine forth in the world with mercy and kindness.
Embraced in wisdom, your acts of compassion
will produce fruit that you might not see,
but I see.
No act of kindness goes unnoticed by Me.
Always, always loving-kindness and tender mercies
produce a bountiful harvest.

MICAH 6:8; LAMENTATIONS 3:22; PSALM 103:17; MATTHEW 5:7, 9:37;
1 CORINTHIANS 6:3; COLOSSIANS 3:12; ROMANS 12:10

My Words for Him

What Hurts Can Make You Strong

Don't be afraid of the fiery opposition that
  comes against you. I'm with you.
The ploys of the enemy are the very instruments
  that I will use to bless, strengthen,
and prosper you.
  I've chosen you to rise above
   the ploys of the enemy,
the enemies of God Almighty,
  in My name.
Through overcoming the clashing, bashing abuse
  of ungodly giants, your spiritual life will be bolstered
and you'll be promoted to higher levels
  of authority and courage.
You'll be impenetrable!
  These giants exist inside and outside you,
   and I want them destroyed
because, dear one, that which was meant for evil
  will be used by Me
to make you great in My Kingdom.

GENESIS 50:20

My Words for Him

In Silence I Speak

Even when I am silent
    I am speaking to you.
My love speaks, My kindness speaks,
    My compassion speaks.
When you look for Me, you'll always
    find Me.
You'll find Me in the fine details
    of a simple dandelion;
you'll see Me in the kindness of a stranger,
    in the thunder of a sunset,
the sweet kiss of a loved one.
    I am the wind,
I am the sun,
    I am every star in the heavens.
I created all and I live in all.
    Listen as I sing to you
the love song of eternity
    with My eye on
the sparrow
    and My heart fixed
on you.

PSALMS 22:2, 33:9, 84:3; JOHN 3:16;
JEREMIAH 31:3; ROMANS 1:20, 8:35

My Words for Him

I Love to Love You

When you awake in the morning
and donate your day to Me,
    can you feel My smile cover you?
When you meet with the challenges of the day
    with a brave heart and faith in Me,
can you feel My hug?
    When you stand strong against temptation,
    can you hear your angels cheer?
I am loving you and enjoying you
    at this very moment, My dear.
Can you sense Me here beside you,
    holding you as the apple of My eye?

I love to love you.
    I love the way you reach into life
to draw out the best,
    the sweetest, and the most enriching
even when it's difficult to do.
    I love the way you embrace the strength
of My Spirit to see your way
    to the goal set before you.
I love your praises lifted to Me
    and I carry them in My heart.
    As your praises multiply
from your heart to Mine,
    your favor multiplies,
and your joy marries Mine.
    Together we soar above every care.

PSALMS 55:22, 88:13, 92:2; ISAIAH 58:8; LAMENTATIONS 3:23;
HEBREWS 2:12; REVELATION 19:5;
DEUTERONOMY 32:10; ZECHARIAH 2:8; JOHN 14:1

My Words for Him

Handling Change

When you see Me at work in the world around you,
     be assured that I am doing a new work in you.
I draw you aside today to tell you that I am bringing new things
     into your life which may challenge you to accept
a fresh way of thinking.
You will find yourself altering the essence
     of your understanding, as old habits, methods, and tools of
understanding will no longer suffice.
You will be required
     to form new attitudes, and enlarge the pegs of the tent
of your thinking.

     Open your spiritual eyes to see Me
as I want to be seen.
     Open your ears to hear Me
as I want to be heard.
     When I speak, you are strengthened.
Do not tremble at change for I am leading you
     perfectly. Nothing is out of order
or wrongly timed. All is perfect.
     I am upsizing the dimensions of your heart and mind
and your sphere of influence. Ask and I will open
     floodgates of wisdom. Follow Me
confidently in this change and
     you and your soul will prosper
as never before.

Psalms 32:8, 10:17; Exodus 23:20; Isaiah 40:20;
1 Kings 3:11-12, 4:29; Esther 4:14; Colossians 1:9;
Ecclesiastes 2:26; James 1:5, 3:17; 3 John 1:2

My Words for Him

The Quiet Place

Your spiritual strength and wisdom
are born in the quiet place with Me.
Allow your thoughts and your many needs
and worries today to hush in the presence of Perfection.
I am your God.
Your peace of mind is here with Me in the quiet place
where I wait for you daily.

I will create a new heart in you as you lean into Mine,
waiting and listening. Let Me comfort you
and stroke your brow. In the multitude of your anxieties,
My comforts will delight your soul.
The whirlwind of your daily life can leave you
wind-swept and disheveled, but here with Me,
you are the portraiture of serenity and calm.
I speak peace to you, to your home, and all
that you possess. When your heart is at peace, you bring
peace to everything around you.

Peace is a fruit of My Holy Spirit,
Which I freely give to you,
and it is My desire that you multiply the fruit
I give you. Your beautiful demeanor
centered in Mine goes far across the world,
by the power of the Holy Spirit,
multiplying My presence wherever you are.
When I say, "Go in peace," I am telling you
to leave all troubles, anxieties, and worries behind,
and wear the confidence of heaven,
for I am your peace.

1 Samuel 25:6; 2 Kings 5:19; Psalms 4:8, 23:2-3, 51:10, 94:19;
Ezekiel 37:26; Jeremiah 29:11

My Words for Him

Eyes to See

I love these moments with you. This is our time to share
    the glow of eternity's radiance and talk
to one another.
    Open the windows of your heart today
to observe the blessings that I have chosen
    to encircle you with.
I am peeling back a corner of heaven for you to peer into–
    yes, heaven on earth!

Open the eyes of your spirit
    to see the blessings that I am pouring out,
blessings you are not accustomed to looking for.
    You have preferred to reach out for the obvious
and I am the Lord of the not-so-obvious,
    which are those things that only the eyes of your spirit
can recognize.

I love to accomplish good for you,
so be aware today of the goodness following you.
    Be aware that all is well.

1 Corinthians 1:9; Genesis 13:14; Deuteronomy 11:7, 28:8;
Psalms 3:8, 13:3, 23:6; Hebrews 6:14

My Words for Him

How to Think of Me

Dearest one, think of Me as your Rock.
 I am the Rock you can stand on,
sit on, lie down on, do cartwheels on, languish on,
 dance on, jump up and down on, and
you're always secure.
 Think of Me as your Fortress
where the walls are impenetrable; no weapon
 has been formed, nor ever will be,
to pierce through to reach you here.
 I am your Rock and your Fortress.

Think of Me as your Shield.
 On the other side of this Shield
furious wars, wild fires, mad dogs,
 and deadly epidemics rage,
but they can't render you helpless because
 My Shield covers you.
I am your Shield.
 I will take the bullet, the sword, the kick in the teeth
for you because I am most of all,
 your Friend
who will never leave you nor forsake you.
 I am your Forever.

2 Samuel 22:1-2; Proverbs 17:17a, 18:24, 27:6a;
Exodus 33:1; Hebrews 13:5; Romans 8:39

My Words for Him

Knowing Your Path

Never consent to becoming a victim
of the world's busy-ness and fussy pursuits.
In the swill and flush of reckless activity, your mind can rinse
itself of the sweet rain of heaven.
Milk and honey flow at your ankles, but when
you set your feet afar off, they trudge about
in a far country, becoming tired, bruised, and calloused
at tasks you weren't called to do.
Oh how I love you! Can you feel My Spirit gently
guiding you to remain on the path
I've prepared just for you?

I am closer than you think, beloved.
Lay aside your agenda for a moment.
Quiet your mind.
Allow your thoughts and your many needs
and worries to hush in the Presence of Perfection.
Hear My thoughts as I speak to you,
and allow My Spirit to do His job.

Your peace will increase in the quiet place
where I wait for you daily. It is not the pressures in life
that are so debilitating, dear one, it is the absence
of My Spirit that wearies the soul.

It matters not what disorder
or trouble swirls around you, I am here,
and your path is sure.
Worldly plans will get you nowhere,
but the Father's plan for your life is eternal
and beautiful.
Stay on the path.

JOHN 6:18; PSALMS 17:4-5; 23:3; PROVERBS 2:8, 3:1-4; JEREMIAH 31:3;
ECCLESIASTES 4:6; EXODUS 14:14; DEUTERONOMY 33:27

My Words for Him

Locked in the Love Heart of God

Quick. Take hold of the door into My love heart;
　　　　jump inside and close the door behind you.
In this set-apart place, I whisper My words into your heart.
　　　　Here in My permanent love heart
with the door closed, you're secure,
　　　　and it's here you'll discover heaven's secrets
and the plans I have for you.

　　　　Understand, My dear one, that
when you are safe in My love heart, nothing can harm you.
　　　　Not pestilence, disease, famine, draught–
nothing. Any voice raised up against you
　　　　will choke as your beauty condemns its sound.
This is your heritage in Me, beloved!
　　　　In My love heart there isn't a weapon
devised that can succeed to touch you.

　　　　Security is rooted inside your heart
where I live locked tight,
　　　　forever your protection and the lover of your soul.

MATTHEW 6:6, 24:33; JOHN 10:1, 7, 9; REVELATION 3:20, 4:1;
PSALMS 9:3, 6, 27:5; DEUTERONOMY 7:13, 29:29, ISAIAH 54:17

My Words for Him

Loved Ones

I hear your prayers.
I hear when you cry out to Me
for your loved ones.
I know the sincerity of your heart
and I know how you think. Sometimes you
worry when you should trust.
I want your loved ones blessed,
healed, and safe in Me, too.

I know you want only the best
for those you love. You want to see them
healed, delivered, saved, and living as you think
best for them.
Is what you think best, or is what I think best?

I want the same as you, dearest child.
When you see your loved ones held captive
in strongholds outside of your help
and control, remember My power is greater,
able to break prison doors,
release captives, and destroy enemies.
I heal and I deliver from bondage.
Your loved ones are in My arms. I love them, too.
I have made a covenant with you,
founded on My purposes, which nothing can hinder.
All that I do is good.
Trust Me.

2 Samuel 22:31; Psalm 9:10; Isaiah 49:25, 65:23-24

My Words for Him

Tenderly Leading

Always remember I love those who love Me,
  and those who seek Me diligently will find
Me.
  Remember I am Wisdom and Knowledge
and Discretion, and I live in you.
  I live in your mind, in your heart, and in your body.
My Holy Spirit is the healing force inside you
  to guide, teach, and anoint you
to recognize and receive the message of My love
  and the path I have set before you
every day.
  I want you to delve into your resolve
to encompass and embrace the course
  I have set before you.
Listen for the sound of My voice deep within you,
  tenderly leading you. I never push or
thump against the sensitive heart tissues of My chosen.
  I tell you today, be prepared
for new things, dearest one.
  I know how you love My Word
and love these precious moments together,
  so I tell you today to open the eyes of your soul
and see Me move in new ways in your life.
  Great rejoicing awaits you.

PROVERBS 8:14, 17, 16:9; DEUTERONOMY 6:5;
PSALM 119:32; GENESIS 22:18, 27:8; 1 CORINTHIANS 5:7;
2 CORINTHIANS 5:17; EPHESIANS 4:24

My Words for Him

_____

_____

_____

_____

_____

_____

_____

_____

_____

_____

_____

_____

_____

_____

_____

_____

_____

You Are Not Alone

You think you are alone in your work
and that no one is helping you.
The truth is you are not alone, and
you have more help than you know.
The armies of heaven are alongside you, dear one.
Your partners in your work are the invisible hosts
whom I've assigned to assist you.

Beloved, I have called you,
and in your work you will prosper greatly.
My angels love success, for they only know
success. They labor beside you gladly,
accepting their task, so I tell you
to be happy, rejoice. You are not alone,
and you will succeed beyond your dreams.

I have appointed an astounding future for you
where you will prove your work
to be masterly led by Me. All that you do
will exhibit more blessings than you can count.
Remain solidly fixed on My purposes, dear one.
Show respect to your angel partners today
by praising Me and rejoicing.

PSALM 68:11, 91:11-12, 145:2; LUKE 2:13;
COLOSSIANS 1:6; 2 KINGS 6:17

My Words for Him

Your Song

In My right hand are pleasures meant just for you.
  I know you, My beloved; I know what stirs
your heart and spreads a smile in your spirit.
  I know the words to your song
because it's the song I wrote for you. You harmonize
  with the angels when you sing your song;
did you know that?
  The ecstasy of union with Me produces
a hymn of blessing and favor so melodious
  the rocks and hills awaken from their slumber,
wipe the sleep from their eyes,
  and join the song.
Like a choir of eager children the whole earth
  raises its voice
to become My voice
  as I call you to do.

  The song is called *faith*, dear one, and faith
has a sound,
  a sound that vibrates
across the endless galaxies of creation
  entering My courts in heaven
where the throne of God inhabits eternity.
  Shall I not open the palm of My hand
to pour out pleasures forevermore to My beloved
  when the sound of your faith throbs
and pulsates across the atmosphere and finds
  its rest in the ears of God?

PSALMS 28:6-8, 35:27, 98:1, 118:4; 2 SAMUEL 22:1;
MATTHEW 9:22, 17:20; 1 CHRONICLES 29:17

My Words for Him

I Am Energizing You

Beloved, this is a time of great growth.
> My Spirit is stretching you.

You may wonder where I am in the events of your life,
> but I am right here.

Listen for My voice. I am continually speaking to you.
> You are My beautiful instrument.

I perform My will upon My instruments.
> You are My treasure, and I want you

to be accustomed to accepting My will in your life
> even when you don't understand it.

Why are young people such effective spiritual warriors?
> Because they have fewer defeats.

Why are My seasoned ones such effective generals?
> Because they've had so many triumphs!

I have already triumphed for you.
> Never ever doubt Me.

Remember My timing is not your timing.
> Your body is My temple.

Where you step your foot, you bring the light of heaven.
> Look with your spiritual eyes to truly see,

and be patient, dear one.
> I am working a great thing in you.

You will know the hope and reality of your calling.
> I am energizing you to accomplish much.

ESTHER 4:13-14; ISAIAH 33:6; 2 CORINTHIANS 4:7;
PSALMS 71:4, 92:14; 1 CORINTHIANS 6:19

My Words for Him

I Fulfill My Promises

Beloved, I am with you.
 I will fulfill My Word concerning you
as I have promised. My Word to you
 in this hour is to stand strong,
stronger than you are accustomed to.
 Understand that the storms of life
prove the power of God within you.
 My promises are perfect and trustworthy
and you have the power to overcome, to rise up
 in strength and prove My Word is true.
Worry will get you nowhere but
 smack into the jaws of the very thing you fear.
I tell you, dear one, you have the power within you
 to experience triumph in *all things*.
Use the authority I give you to boldly proclaim
 the truth of My Word,
My Word which says you can do *all things*
 through Me; My Word which says
I am the strength of your life;
 My Word which says it is I Who works in you
both to will and to do for My good pleasure.
 Contend for My will in the situation facing you.
Stand strong.

Isaiah 43:2-3a; Psalms 27:1, 66:8-10; Romans 8:35-39;
2 Corinthians 5:7; Philippians 2:13, 4:3

My Words for Him

The Goodness That Builds Monuments

I have called you to a life of goodness.

I have called you to a life of blessings and favor.

I have given you My Spirit to enable you to surge beyond outward appearances

to see directly into My heart and mind concerning you.

I don't chain you to Me with harsh demands.

I never condemn you and never wipe your nose in the mud

you're tempted to play in.

I love you with compassion and mercy, and I tell you again,

don't look at outward appearances.

Don't be fooled by what *seems* to be good.

Walk by faith not by sight.

I am not afar off.

I'm right here.

Remember, the devil fakes goodness, and

only he makes demands of you,

driving you to create flimsy castles of mud

when I call you to build entire citadels in gold.

I give you the blueprints!

I live with you in love, dear one.

Allow My love to be the chief elements

permeating your life and the monuments

you long to build.

Psalms 16:2, 23:6, 33:9, 37:34, 121:1-2; Zechariah 9:16; Matthew 7:15; Deuteronomy 13:4

My Words for Him

My Helper

You are looking at the myriad woes and problems
around you, and your heart is troubled.
Your faith is far more precious than gold that perishes,
so do not allow the precious fringes
to tarnish with anxious thoughts.
Do not permit your emotions
to run wild over that which you cannot control.
Pray to Me, the Lord of the Harvest,
and I will anoint you
to bring My love and healing power
into the situations that touch you so deeply.
I will show you the means and the way;
I will help and guide you by My Spirit.
Your passion to help is My passion, too,
but without My guidance, you will flail about
like a child dizzy from twirling
on one toe for too long.
You are appreciated and you are loved
in My Kingdom, and I watch over you
like a mother hen over her chicks.
I do not assign you to a task
without first equipping you to succeed.
Allow Me to equip you. Allow Me to lead you.
Allow Me to kiss your passionate heart
and send you forth empowered.

JAMES 1:3; LUKE 21:19; 2 SAMUEL 22:26;
REVELATION 2:19; JOSHUA 1:2; ISAIAH 6:8, 40:3;
PSALMS 70:4, 100:2; MATTHEW 9:38

My Words for Him

Your Calling

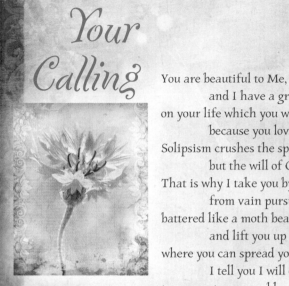

You are beautiful to Me,
    and I have a great and high calling
on your life which you will fulfill
    because you love Me with a true heart.
Solipsism crushes the spirit,
    but the will of God lives forever.
That is why I take you by your precious arm to steer you
    from vain pursuits that render you exhausted and
battered like a moth beating its wings against a sealed window,
    and lift you up into the light
where you can spread your wings and soar with eagles.
    I tell you I will open the windows of heaven
to pour out so many blessings
    you won't be able to contain them all
as you trust Me and honor Me in your calling.
    No chore of yours escapes My watchful eye.
All work you do is sacred and holy to Me.
    I love a thankful heart at work,
for when done in My name, it is a holy calling.

Song of Songs 1:15; Proverbs 16:5, 21:4; Ecclesiastes 4:7;
2 Thessalonians 3:13; Revelation 2:4; Malachi 3:10

My Words for Him

I Know It's Not Easy

Dear one: I am calling you to the banquet hall of mercy
and tender heartedness.
I am calling you to *really know* understanding
and forgiveness.
I know it's difficult to forgive
when those who wrong you are heartless
and cruel. When I was on earth, I learned
the pain of betrayal.
But O, My dearest one, goodness surrounds you
at this moment. You can reach out
and touch My goodness surrounding you, your house,
and all you possess.

My mercy wraps her arms around you, and
wisdom calls you and woos you sweetly and perfectly,
guiding you into My mind and purposes.

Never concern yourself with what they try to take from you
or how they slight and wound you.
You are *Mine*, and I forever bless you and give back to you
a hundredfold what the enemy tries to steal from you,
including your self-esteem and sense of worthiness.

I am speaking directly to your heart, My love;
I am giving you the most precious gift, the gift
of forgiveness.
Forgive, I say. Forgive them.
Nothing has been taken from you except your intent
to rise up stronger than ever.
Nothing and no one can take your worthiness
nor the immense value you are to the Kingdom of God.
Rise up, I say. Rise up!
You're not a foolish plaything for the devil
to toss about in his dirty teeth, shaking you like a toy.
No, dear one, you are a citadel in My courts and I expect you to
rise up, filled with the wisdom of forgiveness,
so you can carry on as the sunshine child I've called you to be.
I love you.

Psalm 118:2; Job 12:3, 28:28; Proverbs 1:2; Matthew 6:12; Isaiah 60:1

My Words for Him

I Am Guiding You

Beloved, I see the decisions that are before you
and I am here to help you.
First, look into your heart and ask yourself
if the choices you make today
can alter the past. What do you see?
When you see that you cannot change
the past, prepare to step into the future
with a solid God-centered intention
to bring forth fruit.
Not all fruit is tangible; at times you
may wonder if you make the right decisions
because you can't see outward benefits
immediately. I am in you to tell you, trust Me.
Trust yourself in Me. Do not fear
the unknown. Be reminded I know everything.
I see everything. I know and Am
the beginning and the end.
Choose to bless Me, My child.
Ask Me for the decision that will bless Me
and bring Me honor.

I have given you My Spirit to guide and help you.
Can you be confident? I am your sun
and your shield. I light the path before you.
Be brave. Be bold.
You have been lifted out of confusion's hot fist.
Now trust the wisdom that I have placed in you.

Deuteronomy 7:13, 30:18-20; Psalms 1:3, 47:4;
Proverbs 3:31; Isaiah 7:15; Job 17:11-12; Song of Songs 2:11;
Exodus 13:20-22; 1 Corinthians 12:8-10

My Words for Him

My Cross and Your Cross

Do you remember I told My disciples that the Father and I
    are *One*? There was nothing on earth or heaven
that I could do without Him.
    Now you, dearest child, on earth,
can do nothing without *Me*.
    Your cross is to deny yourself and follow Me.

I have told you to carry your cross, but
    I have not asked you to carry Mine.
The death on the cross for all human sin
    is My holy sacrifice, not yours.
Your cross is to die to your own sin,
    not the sins of the world.
Pull away from and die to your self-centered
    carnal nature. Be consumed today
with the desire to please Me.
    Your carnal plans and frustrating ambitions
are heavy stones in your shoes; they take you nowhere.
    But oh, My dear, your cross of self-denial
and utter trust is light, not heavy.
    Take a giant leap with your cross into the sacred place
of trust where you will find everything
    you've ever longed for–and more.
Conquer yourself and be free to live fully
    and expressively in Me.
The conquering spirit cannot fail.

John 10:30, 17:11, 21, 19:19; Galatians 6:14;
Hebrews 12:2; Matthew 6:24; Romans 8:37

That Which Awaits You

Beloved one, you have asked for My will
and My leading in your life.
I am answering you.
I bring new things into your life.
You are about to discover
your heart and mind expanding
into new territories of faith.
Always remember I love those who love Me.
Those who seek Me diligently will find Me.
Remember I am Wisdom and Knowledge
and Discretion.
I live in you.
I live in your mind, in your heart,
and in your body.
My Holy Spirit is the healing, guiding force inside you.
He is teaching and anointing you to understand
and love My ways.
Be prepared, I say.
Open the eyes of your heart
and see Me move in new ways in your life.
Great prosperity awaits you.

PROVERBS 2:11, 8:14, 17; PHILIPPIANS 2:13;
DEUTERONOMY 7:9; JEREMIAH 33:3; ECCLESIASTES 9:10;
ISAIAH 11:2; PSALM 112:5; JOSHUA 1:8

My Words for Him

My Words for Him

My Words for Him

My Words for Him

My Words for Him

My Words for Him

My Words for Him

MARIE CHAPIAN, New York Times best-selling author, has published more than 30 books translated into 17 languages. Recipient of many awards including the coveted Gold Medallion Book Award, she is a certified Christian life coach, pastor, spiritual director, and award-winning poet and artist Marie holds a doctorate in counseling, an MFA in writing, and is founder and president of JC Wings of Wellness–a ministry dedicated to spirit, soul, and body wholeness. She is passionate for the loving heart of God to illuminate the human heart with His compassion, joy, and peace. Her ministry stretches across several continents bringing the transforming majesty of His words to all who will listen. Visit her at www.mariechapian.com.